PRAYER MADE EASY

PRAYER MADE EASY

7 Moves That Simplify Prayer

DEVOTIONAL

JEFF McAFFEE

RESOURCE *Publications* • Eugene, Oregon

PRAYER MADE EASY
7 Moves That Simplify Prayer: Devotional

Copyright © 2023 Jeff McAffee. All rights reserved. Except for brief quotations in critical publications or reviews, no part of this book may be reproduced in any manner without prior written permission from the publisher. Write: Permissions, Wipf and Stock Publishers, 199 W. 8th Ave., Suite 3, Eugene, OR 97401.

Resource Publications
An Imprint of Wipf and Stock Publishers
199 W. 8th Ave., Suite 3
Eugene, OR 97401

www.wipfandstock.com

PAPERBACK ISBN: 978-1-6667-6040-8
HARDCOVER ISBN: 978-1-6667-6041-5
EBOOK ISBN: 978-1-6667-6042-2

01/04/23

Scripture quotations marked (ESV) are from The ESV® Bible (The Holy Bible, English Standard Version®), copyright © 2001 by Crossway, a publishing ministry of Good News Publishers. Used by permission. All rights reserved.

Scripture quotations marked (NIV) are taken from the Holy Bible, New International Version®, NIV®. Copyright © 1973, 1978, 1984, 2011 by Biblica, Inc.™ Used by permission of Zondervan. All rights reserved worldwide. www.zondervan.com The "NIV" and "New International Version" are trademarks registered in the United States Patent and Trademark Office by Biblica, Inc.™

Scripture quotations marked (NLT) are taken from the Holy Bible, New Living Translation, copyright ©1996, 2004, 2015 by Tyndale House Foundation. Used by permission of Tyndale House Publishers, Carol Stream, Illinois 60188. All rights reserved.

This book is dedicated to everyone who longs
for prayer to be simpler in their life.

CONTENTS

Acknowledgments   ix
Introduction   xi

Entering the Throne Room | Your First Move   1

Day 1: God is All-Powerful   3
Day 2: God is Ever Present   5
Day 3: God Is a Promise Keeper   7
Day 4: God is Sovereign   9

Laying Yourself on the Altar | Your Second Move   11

Day 5: Renewal of Mind   13
Day 6: The Strength of Weaknesses   15
Day 7: I Am a New Creation   17
Day 8: I Am Valuable   19
Day 9: Stay Humble   21
Day 10: Come Closer   23

Guarding Your Sanctuary | Your Third Move   25

Day 11: A House Dedicated   27
Day 12: Let's Get Real About Love   29
Day 13: Promise for the Children   31
Day 14: Praying for Someone in Danger   33
Day 15: The Power of Mutual Submission   35
Day 16: A Peaceful Habitation   37

Contents

Connecting With Your Tribe | Your Fourth Move — 39
- Day 17: Brotherly Affection — 41
- Day 18: Love Has a Face — 43
- Day 19: A Cool Drink — 45
- Day 20: The Labor of New Life — 47
- Day 21: Dinner with Friends — 49
- Day 22: Thank God for Good Friends! — 51

Worshiping in the Tabernacle | Your Fifth Move — 53
- Day 23: Active Worship — 55
- Day 24: A Good Stir — 57
- Day 25: One Bread, One Body — 59
- Day 26: Love at Risk — 61
- Day 27: Oh, How He Loves Us! — 63
- Day 28: The Living Body — 65

Showing Love in the Marketplace | Your Sixth Move — 67
- Day 29: Wrecking Ball Love — 69
- Day 30: A Prayer for Our Neighborhood — 71
- Day 31: Making the Cut — 73
- Day 32: Three Powerful Words — 75
- Day 33: Being Witnesses — 77
- Day 34: The Ouch of Forgiveness — 79

Going to the Highways and Byways | Your Seventh Move — 81
- Day 35: The Ripe Harvest — 83
- Day 36: Right Place. Right Time. — 85
- Day 37: The Seedbed of Opportunity — 87
- Day 38: This Little Light of Mine — 89
- Day 39: Identify Fidelity — 91
- Day 40: The Right Move — 93

Conclusion — 95
About the Author — 97

ACKNOWLEDGMENTS

Special thanks to Pastor Stacy Valenzuela and Pastor Missie Richardson who work with me at The Well Church for their contributions to this devotional. Pastor Stacy wrote the devotions for day fifteen and for day thirty-three, and also served as the editor for this book. Tremendous gratitude for her excellent editorial work (I owe her a new red pen). Pastor Missie wrote the devotion for day thirteen. We all wish they could have written more! You'll enjoy their point of view. Special thanks to Deanne Welsh for showing me to maneuver through the world of writing. Special thanks for my wife, Kendra, and our kids Ethan, Anna, and Ella, for their continued love and support.

INTRODUCTION

It took several years until it finally clicked. I believed in Jesus. I went to church and was involved. But I didn't know how to pray. I struggled, fumbled, and faked it whenever trying to pray privately. And publicly? That just wasn't happening. Why was it that others could pray with eloquence, sounding so great while my prayers sounded like the unsaved teenager trying to pray for dinner?

Shouldn't this come naturally? Why wasn't it working for me?

The prayer person I am today, however, is quite different. Confident and competent are better words of description. Knowing what to say comes more naturally. I can pray publicly or with other people. Praying alone with just me and God is enjoyable.

I first became interested in prayer when, as a minister, I realized this key part of being a Christian was missing from my life. I was starting to feel like a hypocrite.

I now understand a few important and life-transformative principles about prayer. One, learning how to become a seasoned prayer person doesn't take long. Two, it doesn't have to be difficult. And three, each prayer move is easy to understand and remember.

THE MOVES

Yes, prayer is about moves. This book will lead you through the seven moves of prayer that will transform your prayer life into one that flows and helps you connect with the heart of God. We begin

Introduction

with the first move of focusing on the exaltation of God and then move into the second move of bringing all of ourselves before Him.

The third move shifts to our home and immediate family. Our spouse, kids, and anyone else. This move brings them into focus. What if we're alone in the house? No worries. We pray for the ones who used to be with us but are now out on their own. We pray for the ones who should be there but are missing

The fourth and fifth moves draw attention to extended family and friends and to our church. Grandparents, nieces and nephews, cousins, and all the rest. And, what about our friends? What are their names? We might be the only person in the world praying for them. Our pastors need prayer. The volunteers, programs, and ministries do, too. What kinds of needs exist here?

The sixth and seventh moves reach out to our community and the world. This includes the places, organizations, and people we are involved with outside of our homes and churches. Who are our coworkers, classmates, store and restaurant employees you visit regularly? Like us, they have needs and some are stuck in circumstances where they need divine wisdom.

THE INVITATIONS

Each devotion ends with an invitation for divine self-reflection and prayer. While each devotion guides our prayer life through the seven moves, the invitations of divine self-reflection equip us to implement and move forward confidently.

The invitations beckon us to love incarnationally. They take the agape love of Christ that exists within us and enrobes it with the flesh of our hands, feet, and words. Something powerful happens when the moves of our hearts become tangible. We become Jesus to the world around us.

Included with the invitations is an opportunity for you to write, by hand, the verse of the devotion in the space provided. This creates a special time of divine reflection and prayer.

Are you ready? Let's dive in.

Entering the Throne Room

YOUR FIRST MOVE

What fills the throne room of God? Worship! When Isaiah was ushered into the presence of God by the Spirit, he witnessed worship taking place in its purest form. Overcome, he fell and immediately professed his sinfulness as an offering. He began to worship.

The worship of God is the starting place of prayer. If someone asked us to explain God, we would probably start by talking about how God is big, strong, and powerful, and that kind of stuff. We would probably share about how God is loving, caring, and compassionate. We might even describe his creativity and power, as the One who created the heavens and the earth. All of this is true.

When God is worshiped through prayer, *the things we know to be true about him are declared as an offering of prayer.* Everything we just said about God is declared as prayer.

Why is this important and why is this a necessary first move of prayer? Our declarations of God's greatness reposition us in submission to his authority and re-orients our thinking back to alignment with God's thinking. Our will gets reset to his will. Our thoughts sync with his thoughts. Our passions are set ablaze by his passions.

This kind of prayerful worship of God re-centers us into proper alignment with God. Effective prayers are those in line with God's plans and heart. The secret to effective prayers is not praying what we want, or what we think is needed for a person or situation. Instead, it's joining in on how the Spirit is already praying for us.

Worship of God through prayer is the first move because it ushers us into the throne room of God and re-focuses our gaze upon the only one who can answer us and who is already at work for us. Without it, we may never get out of the starting gate. We begin with declarations of praise, thankfulness, and gratitude for who God is and what He has done.

The first four devotions of our journey begin with entering into the throne room with declarations of praise.

Day 1

GOD IS ALL-POWERFUL

But Jesus looked at them and said, "With man this is impossible, but with God all things are possible."
MATTHEW 19:26 (ESV)

As we pray today, let's thank God that he creates beautiful things out of nothing. He creates order out of chaos. He loves and cares for us. He is powerful enough to take care of all our needs.

The universe is about ninety-three billion light-years across from edge to edge. God created the whole universe out of nothing but his spoken word. If God can create the universe out of nothing, just imagine what he can create in our lives! As we pray on this today, let's thank God for how powerful he is and how he takes care of our needs!

Jesus told the crowds that God loves us so much that even the hairs of our head are numbered. What great comfort we have in knowing that if God promises to take care of little birds who have little worth that he will care for us, who have infinitely greater value. Even the most important need is cared for by God. . .our relationship with him.

The disciples wondered in amazement at how it would be possible for a rich man to enter the Kingdom of God. Jesus eased their fears. What seems like an impossibility to man is possible with God. All things are possible with God. Do we believe this today?

THE INVITATION

As you're praying today, identify two reasons to thank God for how powerful he has been in your life. Take a moment to write them down as a remembrance for yourself and then choose someone to share them with today.

DIVINE REFLECTION AND PRAYER

In the space below, and in your own hand, write out Matthew 19:26. As you do, reflect upon the invitation, and pray.

Day 2

GOD IS EVER PRESENT

Where shall I go from your Spirit?
Or where shall I flee from your presence?
If I ascend to heaven, you are there!
If I make my bed in Sheol, you are there!

PSALM 139:7–8 (ESV)

God is both transcendent and immanent. He is both far and near. He existed before he created the heavens and the earth, and all space and time and dimension. He is bigger than our universe, and yet he is close at hand. He knows the number of hairs on our heads.

As we pray today, let's thank God that we are never alone and that God's presence is with us everywhere we go!

David knew this truth well. He called upon God to be with him as he fought off bears and lions. God was with him on many lonely shepherd nights as he wrote songs and poetry. The presence of God was with him as Israel's greatest king. And God was especially close with him even in all his failures.

God is always with us and will never leave us. What would it look like if we believed this truth? Even in our most difficult and darkest times, he's there. When we think he's abandoned us, he hasn't.

Some of the most profound healing for believers comes when we can recognize that God has always been there, and he always will be.

THE INVITATION

What's a great hurt you've experienced in your life? Did you know Jesus was there while it was happening? Look again in your memory's eye. Do you see him? He saw the whole thing. He was with you. Healing starts when you take your hurt to him. He wants it. He's ready for it. He's the only one who can heal you.

DIVINE REFLECTION AND PRAYER

In the space below, and in your own hand, write out Psalm 139:7–8. As you do, reflect upon the invitation, and pray.

Day 3

GOD IS A PROMISE KEEPER

I prayed to the LORD my God and made confession, saying, "O Lord, the great and awesome God, who keeps covenant and steadfast love with those who love him and keep his commandments,

DANIEL 9:4 (ESV)

Daniel had been fervently praying and fasting for the Israelites, his people. They had landed in trouble and had been carried off into Babylonian captivity. He prayed for God to forgive them and to restore them to their land and to rebuild their Temple.

Daniel knew God would respond to his prayer because *God is a promise keeper*. Do you believe He is a promise keeper?

Daniel showed us that the secret to successful prayers is found in praying God's promises. There are hundreds of promises in the Bible. Here are a few to consider:

> God Is Our Guide: I *will instruct you and teach you in the way you should go; I will counsel you with my eye upon you.* Psalm 32:8 (ESV)

> God Is with Us: *Fear not, for I am with you; be not dismayed, for I am your God; I will strengthen you, I will*

help you, I will uphold you with my righteous right hand. Isaiah 41:10 (ESV)

God Works Everything Out: *And we know that for those who love God all things work together for good, for those who are called according to his purpose.* Romans 8:28 (ESV)

THE INVITATION

Where do you need God to fulfill one of his promises in your life today? Is it a relationship? Job? Health or unresolved conflict? Deliverance from a stronghold? The Bible has a promise for every situation. *Pray about this situation today.* Search for some verses about these needs. Let's bring these needs to the Lord.

DIVINE REFLECTION AND PRAYER

In the space below, and in your own hand, write out Daniel 9:4. As you do, reflect upon the invitation, and pray.

DAY 4

GOD IS SOVEREIGN

For, at just the right time Christ will be revealed from heaven by the blessed and only almighty God, the King of all kings and Lord of all lords.

1 TIMOTHY 6:15 (NLT)

I don't like being late for events. I don't like the lack-of-care message it communicates. The truth is, I *do* care. But sometimes I have situations that keep me from keeping time with my calendar.

God, however, is an on-time God! There's nothing that keeps him. God has no jurisdiction over him. He is supreme. He is the highest authority of all creation. That means he has the absolute right to do as he wills. He has no external restraints. He has all power. He is all-knowing and is ever-present. His decrees are irrevocable.

God has decrees for us. God has plans for us. As we pray and meditate today, let's thank God that he is in charge and declare afresh that he is our Lord.

When Paul wrote this verse to Timothy, he was charging him to hold on to his faith until the return of Jesus Christ, whom God would send in his own time. Timothy—as well as us—needed to be reminded that *God is sovereign*.

Like us, Timothy had challenges working against him that tempted him to lose faith and to doubt God's calling. He was young and inexperienced. He was thrust into a role of leadership that he wasn't ready for. His only hope for success was his faith and reliance upon a sovereign God, the King of all kings and Lord of all lords.

God's sovereignty works in accordance with his divine purpose and plans, which includes his will for our lives.

THE INVITATION

What kind of mountain are you facing in your life today? Today's the day to quit trying to move that mountain on your own and rely on the only one who can move it for you. Set a reminder every hour today to pray for God's sovereignty to reign in your life.

DIVINE REFLECTION AND PRAYER

In the space below, and in your own hand, write out 1 Timothy 6:15. As you do, reflect upon the invitation, and pray.

Laying Yourself on the Altar

YOUR SECOND MOVE

The second move in simplifying prayer is all about you. This is where things get personal. The second move is one of the easiest times of prayer because we know who we are and we know what our needs are. It's also, if one is not careful, where we can get bogged down with an over-emphasis on ourselves and forget about others.

Prayer during the second move focuses on two things about ourselves. One, the sin God wants to remove from our lives. And two, the righteousness God wants to impart into our lives. This move flows naturally from our worship we were just experiencing in the first move. This move is a time of confession, cleansing, emptying, and filling. What is God doing in our lives? What is he removing? What is he adding? All these things come into view during this move, and in the context of worship established in the first move.

Identifying the bad things in our lives is easy. These include our sins, bad habits, addictions and strongholds, and the things working against us. The second move of prayer invites us to see ourselves in the divine light of worship, and to ask God to forgive, cleanse, and deliver us of what is being revealed. We see this in Jesus' story about praying in Luke 18, where Jesus describes two men praying at the altar, a Pharisee and a tax collector. It was the tax collector, with his head hung low, beating his chest and crying out to God for forgiveness, that went home justified. The second move allows us to see the truth about ourselves. Sometimes, like the tax collector, it's a time of divine repentance.

This is also a time of God informing us of the things he has for us. The altar of worship is the sacred space of divine stirrings and yearnings for holy things. It's a time where the righteousness of God is imparted into the depths of the believer's soul. There's no other place from which the praying person can obtain the desire for holy things. These moments become the building block moments that transform the believer.

Some people think praying for themselves is selfish. They're wrong. I'm a better dad to my kids when I am first a better husband to my wife. Likewise, I am a better husband to my wife when I am first a better man to myself. And I am the best man possible when I am a better son to Christ. Same with you.

The devotions over the next six days are designed to help you move into the right posture of praying for yourself.

Day 5

RENEWAL OF MIND

Do not be conformed to this world, but be transformed by the renewal of your mind, that by testing you may discern what is the will of God, what is good and acceptable and perfect.

ROMANS 12:2 (ESV)

One of the most difficult challenges facing Christians is the renewal of their mind. It's a common struggle of waffling back and forth between their Christian life and their old life. Some days are "Jesus" days filled with going to church, listening to Christian music, and Bible reading. Other days are "old life" days filled with walking backward, headed towards the counterfeit ways that used to define life.

Paul's challenge to the Roman Christians was to quit allowing the world to shape them and to instead allow Christ to renew their mind. *This is the precursor to the transformed life.* How does this work? Paul told them the key to this was to deny the body (by making it a living sacrifice) while positioning the mind for renewal.

Here's a good illustration. Pickles. Do you like pickles? Once a cucumber has been immersed into vinegar, it becomes permanently transformed into a delicious, crunchy pickle. There's no turning back for the cucumber. No reversal of effect. The cucumber has become a new creation. Renewal of the mind is a permanent transformation.

THE INVITATION

What areas of your mind need this kind of permanent transformation? Is there a specific part of your mind still focused on the life you've left behind? Are you still fixating in areas where need deliverance? As you pray today, ask God to renew your thinking. Let today be the first day of a completely changed mind.

DIVINE REFLECTION AND PRAYER

In the space below, and in your own hand, write out Romans 12:2. As you do, reflect upon the invitation, and pray.

Day 6

THE STRENGTH OF WEAKNESSES

But he said to me, "My grace is sufficient for you, for my power is made perfect in weakness." Therefore I will boast all the more gladly of my weaknesses, so that the power of Christ may rest upon me. For the sake of Christ, then, I am content with weaknesses, insults, hardships, persecutions, and calamities. For when I am weak, then I am strong.

2 CORINTHIANS 12:9–10 (ESV)

Sometimes God allows weaknesses to exist in our lives. Sometimes he refuses to remove them. The good news in this is that God's sovereignty, combined with his intrinsic moral perfection, guarantees that if God refuses to remove such weaknesses in our lives, there is a divinely moral reason he's allowed them to remain.

What does this mean? It means our weaknesses are the places where God's grace is applied. Our weaknesses are met by his strength; our inabilities are met by his ability. Our places of weakness are the places where we become strong. Here's a great maxim: *Whenever great things are accomplished in the Kingdom, God always uses those who know they don't stand a chance without him.*

This is a good position for us to be in. And this is God's design. Paul had a thorn in the flesh (a weakness) that three times he asked

God to remove. Each time God said, "My grace is sufficient for you." Paul knew God sent the thorn to keep him humble. This did two things for Paul. One, it forced Paul to continuously come to God for strength. And two, it never allowed Paul to take credit for the amazing work God was doing through him.

THE INVITATION

What are your weaknesses? That whole part about continuously coming to God for strength. . .this is God's plan for allowing some of these "thorns" to remain in your life. You need God's strength (not yours). Let today be a day of fresh resolve of seeking God in your weaknesses.

DIVINE REFLECTION AND PRAYER

In the space below, and in your own hand, write out 2 Corinthians 12:9–10. As you do, reflect upon the invitation, and pray.

Day 7

I AM A NEW CREATION

Therefore, if anyone is in Christ, he is a new creation. The old has passed away; behold, the new has come.
2 CORINTHIANS 5:17 (ESV)

Being in Christ is an all-in relationship. Nothing hidden. Nothing held back. The two have become one. This is why Paul uses the analogy of marriage to describe our relationship with Jesus. Being in Christ is a covenant vow. Here's a question to start the day: Are we married to Christ or have we only been dating?

Being in Christ is not possible while still holding to our old life. The double life is incompatible with the vow of two becoming one. We can't have both. If we're still committed to living our old life, then we're not committed to Christ. We're not in Christ. We're a Christian in name only and Jesus is only an accessory in our life.

The good news is that if we've given our heart to Christ, we may not be perfect, but we have become a new creation. The Greek word for "creation" here is the same word used for the creation of the world.

That means in the same way that God created the world out of nothing, he has created a new life for us that has nothing to do with our old selves. For every day of creation, God said it was 'good'. You are good!

Are you married to Christ today? Or are you only dating? There are no "girlfriends" of Christ in heaven, only his bride.

THE INVITATION

If I bumped into you in heaven, what would you look like? What would you sound like? What would your personality be like? What kind of work would you be doing? *This is you as a new creation. This is what God wants you to look like today.*

DIVINE REFLECTION AND PRAYER

In the space below, and in your own hand, write out 2 Corinthians 5:17. As you do, reflect upon the invitation, and pray.

Day 8

I AM VALUABLE

Are not two sparrows sold for a penny? And not one of them will fall to the ground apart from your Father. But even the hairs of your head are all numbered. Fear not, therefore; you are of more value than many sparrows.

MATTHEW 10:29–31 (ESV)

God created us. He created us for a purpose. Within that purpose is a divine identity, personality, intellect, and disposition. Many people live their lives totally disconnected from these foundational truths about themselves. They live fraudulent lives of imposter identities.

They're never happy. Of course, they aren't. The good news is that it doesn't have to be this way. We never have to struggle with identity when we can simply go to the one who created us and who will help us generously to walk in that identity.

God knows everything about us. His knowledge about us is perfect and complete. He knows our past, present, and future. Nothing is hidden from God. He knows all our actions, our thoughts, our needs, our struggles. . .everything. God is never surprised with us. He never learns anything new about us because he already knows it all. . .the good, the bad, and the ugly.

And for all that God knows about us, He still says we are His most-prized possession. Who do you value more than anyone or anything else in the world? Who's the one you would die for without thinking? That's how God feels about us.

THE INVITATION

Do you believe you are God's prized possession? And that Jesus will protect and provide for you? As you pray today, sit for a while with this beautiful truth of how much God loves and values you.

DIVINE REFLECTION AND PRAYER

In the space below, and in your own hand, write out Matthew 10:29–31. As you do, reflect upon the invitation, and pray.

Day 9

STAY HUMBLE

Humble yourselves, therefore, under the mighty hand of God so that at the proper time he may exalt you.

1 PETER 5:6 (ESV)

Being humble before the Lord is always the best starting place for prayer. God is sovereign, almighty, and all-knowing. Though God's love for us is great, *he's not our buddy*. He is our Father, and he loves us with the best kind of fatherly love. But, God is not our friend in any way that allows us to relate to him outside the context of him being Sovereign King in our lives.

Humility recognizes this and it rejoices in it. Humility recognizes God's lordship in our lives. It remembers the vow we took when we gave our heart to Christ.

It acknowledges God's mighty hand that protects, leads, provides, and disciplines us. It says, "You are my God. I belong to you. You're in charge."

God's love for us compels Him to adore us. He wants to shower us with abundant blessings. He wants us to be shining examples of what it means to belong to him.

His timing is perfect, and he knows exactly when to pour out these blessings. How does he know we're ready? How do we know when we're ready? We're ready when God gets the glory in our lives and not us.

THE INVITATION

Do you give God credit for all your successes? Today, as you pray, ask God to help you be a humble person. Ask him to make it permanent.

DIVINE REFLECTION AND PRAYER

In the space below, and in your own hand, write out 1 Peter 5:6. As you do, reflect upon the invitation, and pray.

Day 10

COME CLOSER

Let us then with confidence draw near to the throne of grace, that we may receive mercy and find grace to help in time of need.

HEBREWS 4:16 (ESV)

It's ironic how our fallen human nature drives us away from God when we need him the most. This compulsion is called shame. It's a direct result of sin and the devil loves it. Shame tells us that we don't deserve God's grace because of what we've done or how we're being tempted.

But the Spirit speaks a different message. The Spirit tells us that we can overcome these devil-emanating scripts. When our fallen flesh tells us to stay away from God, *these are the times we need to run to God.* The Bible tells us his throne room is always open. Do you believe this? We never need to knock.

What we need most is waiting there: mercy and grace.

The writer of Hebrews wrote these words in context of the struggles we face with temptations. The Bible tells us that Jesus understands every single one of them.

Because of this glorious truth, we never have to think that Jesus will recoil in disgust when we go to him for help. The total opposite is what we're going to find. In the throne room we find compassion, understanding, and help.

THE INVITATION

Have you been avoiding God because of shame? Today, take your temptations and every other reason why you avoid God directly into his throne room. Show them to him and ask for the help you've been needing for a long time.

DIVINE REFLECTION AND PRAYER

In the space below, and in your own hand, write out Hebrews 4:16. As you do, reflect upon the invitation, and pray.

Guarding Your Sanctuary

YOUR THIRD MOVE

The third move brings into focus our homes and the people we live with. This is our safe place, our sanctuary. And these are our spouses, our kids, moms, dads, siblings, and anyone else who lives with us. This is a move that shifts our prayers from the worship of God and praying for self to praying for others. It's a big move. It starts with our closest relationships first and then moves relationally outwards.

If you're married, this move begins with praying for your spouse and from there it moves out to children and anyone else living in the house. If we live alone, no worries, we pray for the sanctity of our home. We pray for its protection and that it would be a habitation of God's Spirit. We pray for our closest family members.

What is God doing with our spouse? The best way to pray for them is the same way we pray for ourselves: body, soul, and spirit. Starting with their body, we pray for health, healing, strength, and vitality. A person's soul consists of their mind, will, emotions, personality, and intellect. For these things we pray for clarity, authenticity, and balance. When praying for a person's spirit, we pray simply and passionately that their spirit is in line with the Spirit of God. We can also pray for their specific needs and listen for how the Spirit is guiding us to pray for needs we may not know. The next six devotions will teach us how to do this.

Day 11

A HOUSE DEDICATED

"...But as for me and my household, we will serve the Lord."
JOSHUA 24:15 (NIV)

Here's a question, if someone walked into your home today, would they know a follower of Jesus lived there? Even though many others will choose to live a different life, can we, like Joshua, declare that our home is a Christian home that belongs to the Lord?

What does it mean that our household is dedicated to serving the Lord? It means that we belong to God, our family belongs to God, and our home belongs to God. In other words, our family and the home in which we live, *is distinctly Christian.*

It means we have a family and a home that looks like a Christian home, feels like a Christian home, has an "atmosphere" of Christianity, and is marked by Christian beliefs, attitudes, and behaviors.

Is this accomplished through decorations? No. It's accomplished through the presence of God's Spirit in us and in the people who live with us.

How should we be praying for the people in our immediate family? What are their needs? Is there any part of our household that needs to be removed? Is there anything that needs to be added?

Joshua's declaration confronted the entire nation of Israel. He was saying, "In every measure of authority in my life and family, my household will be a household that belongs to the Lord." He drew a line in the sand and invited the whole nation to do the same. If we had been there to hear his final speech, how would we have responded?

THE INVITATION

Is your home a distinctly Christian home? Make today a day of fresh resolve for you and your family. Today, and over the next six days, pray for your family and home like you never have before. These devotions will show you the way.

DIVINE REFLECTION AND PRAYER

In the space below, and in your own hand, write out Joshua 24:15. As you do, reflect upon the invitation, and pray.

Day 12

LET'S GET REAL ABOUT LOVE

Love is patient and kind; love does not envy or boast; it is not arrogant or rude. It does not insist on its own way; it is not irritable or resentful; it does not rejoice at wrongdoing, but rejoices with the truth. Love bears all things, believes all things, hopes all things, endures all things.

1 CORINTHIANS 13:4–7 (ESV)

Is this what love looks like in our lives? How different is this biblical definition of love from ours? So often we define love as a feeling. And then when those feelings begin to fade we think we've "fallen out of love." How immature! This is the wrong definition of love. *Love is not a feeling.*

Love is an action. Love is a choice. Love and feelings are mutually exclusive. Though they may enjoy falling in sync with one another, they are not dependent upon one another. The words and actions of love flow not out of feeling but out of disposition.

At its essence, love is the very presence and person of Jesus Christ, who is love, who is the author of love, who is love personified.

Do you remember the first time you experienced the love of Jesus? If you're like me, you probably wept, overcome with the affection God has for you. I'll bet it changed you, even transformed you.

I'll bet it made you want to drop everything and give your heart to Jesus, follow after him, and give him your all. It was probably the very moment your life changed.

THE INVITATION

How much do the people in your home/immediate family need to experience that kind of love? Today, as you pray for your home/immediate family, ask God to transform the love you have for them into a biblical love. Be Jesus to them.

DIVINE REFLECTION AND PRAYER

In the space below, and in your own hand, write out 1 Corinthians 13:4–7. As you do, reflect upon the invitation, and pray.

Day 13

PROMISE FOR THE CHILDREN

All your children shall be taught by the LORD,
and great shall be the peace of your children.
ISAIAH 54:13 (ESV)

From Pastor Missie Richardson.
The first time I read Isaiah 54, I was begging God to comfort my grieving soul. I was twenty-four, had just gone through a painful divorce and was now the single mom of a three year old and a newborn. I couldn't imagine survival, let alone raising them to be healthy, whole and above all else, know Jesus. I knew the statistics and I felt helpless. And then I read Isaiah 54. This chapter speaks so much promise for those with broken lives and hurting families. It starts out directed to a woman who has been abandoned. It speaks of God's great compassion and how He is going to rebuild her life.

What a beautiful moment, where God drew my attention to a truth every parent, teacher, aunt and uncle needs as we seek to influence and raise children who love the Lord. While it was a prophetic message for Israel, it is also a word spoken directly to us. A promise that says that because He loves us, because He has compassion for us, He will rebuild our lives, and we just read in verse thirteen, he will teach our children.

The burden isn't on us alone, but He says that our children will be "taught by the Lord, and great will be their peace." He uses us, as He teaches them through our lives lived before him, how we speak and treat others and even the way that we made mistakes (I made so many mistakes) and clean them up. He teaches them at church, through pastors and leaders and classes. He's teaching them through hardships and tough consequences. He is moving through our prayers and standing strong in our faith. We don't always know what they need to build their faith in him, but He does. And He is teaching them.

THE INVITATION

How are your kids doing today? Honestly. Are they okay? Pray for your kids today. They are loved deeply by the Lord. He sees them and it is his great desire for them to know him. And because of that, we can all have great peace!

DIVINE REFLECTION AND PRAYER

In the space below, and in your own hand, write out Isaiah 54:13. As you do, reflect upon the invitation, and pray.

Day 14

PRAYING FOR SOMEONE IN DANGER

For I will pour water on the thirsty land and streams on the dry ground; I will pour out my Spirit on your offspring, and my blessing on your descendants.

ISAIAH 44:3 (ESV)

There was once a season in my life where my mother feared for my safety. It was many years ago before I had become a Christian. I was lost and doing the things lost boys do. But my mother was a praying mother and she had praying friends! And as she prayed day after day, the Lord gave her two promises. The first was a simple image of me standing, smiling, holding a Bible. The second was a verse from Proverbs that said, "The seed of the righteous shall be delivered (11:21)." She clung to these promises until God delivered me out of that dark season in my life.

The promises in this verse were made from a loving God to a praying prophet. Isaiah constantly spoke to and listened to God. I hope you don't miss this important fact about him. *Isaiah was a praying prophet.* Are you a praying parent? Are you a praying daughter or son?

Sometimes we wonder why God isn't saying anything. If you're not praying, *God is wondering the same thing about you!*

Is there anyone in our home in danger? Here's a life-changing confrontation: Are we remembering that praying for them has the power make them parched and thirsty for God?

My mother rejoiced when she saw me thirsty. She gave me a drink. More importantly, she took me to the well and told me I could drink from it as much as I wanted.

THE INVITATION

Who, in your home, is in danger right now? Today's the day we go to battle for them. Pray for them today. Ask God to make them parched and thirsty.

DIVINE REFLECTION AND PRAYER

In the space below, and in your own hand, write out Isaiah 44:3. As you do, reflect upon the invitation, and pray.

Day 15

THE POWER OF MUTUAL SUBMISSION

Submit to one another out of reverence for Christ.
EPHESIANS 5:21 (ESV)

From Pastor Stacy Valenzuela.
    The word "submit" can be a tough one to swallow. Some of us have been hurt by submitting to someone. Others can't submit because their pride is in the way. Some of us want to submit. We really do. Kind of.
    Here's the truth: submission is a behavior that we must choose. We submit to the law when we stop at a red light. We submit to the alarm when we get up in the morning. But submitting to one another out of reverence for Christ is something bigger than our behavior. *This calls for the heart to get on board.*
    First of all, we are submitting to one another out of reverence for Christ. The whole purpose is to honor our Father in Heaven...to respect Him above all else. I don't know about anybody else, but I've learned how easy things are when there's purpose behind it! And if that purpose involves my Father, well then, count me in!
    Perhaps the toughest people to submit to are those closest to us. But these are also the people that we need to submit to the most.

We need to lay down our need to be right and hear what our loved ones are saying. We need to surrender our selfish desires so that we can see the needs of those that God has placed in our lives. It may hurt; we may not get what we want when we want it; but this is a great way to send a powerful message to those we love.

Submission might look very different than we may imagine but no matter what, it looks like love to Jesus.

THE INVITATION

Are you willing to give this a try? Let's start today!

First, find a loved one who just seems to know how to push your buttons (go big or go home, right?).

Now, ask God to show you where you can submit to them.

It may be that they get to choose the show you watch on TV, what you have for dinner, whether or not you make your bed. It may look like making someone's lunch, making the first move at restoring a relationship, sending a note, or making a phone call. No matter what your submission may look like, God sees your heart, and your heart is to honor Him. Oh, how your submission will please your Father!

DIVINE REFLECTION AND PRAYER

In the space below, and in your own hand, write Ephesians 5:21. As you do, reflect upon the invitation, and pray.

Day 16

A PEACEFUL HABITATION

My people will abide in a peaceful habitation, in secure dwellings, and in quiet resting places.

ISAIAH 32:18 (ESV)

When was the last time you chilled out in a hammock? There you were, swaying away with your sunglasses and hat. Book in one hand; lemonade in the other. Blissfully checked out. Ah yes, it almost makes you want to go swing in one right now, doesn't it?

The Bible says the Spirit of God creates for us a *peaceful habitation*. That doesn't mean we become hammock dwellers, but it does mean that where the Spirit of God is, there is order, there is security, there is quietness, and there is rest.

When it comes to our home, our sanctuary, the focus of this peaceful habitation is not the arrangement of furniture. *The focus is the influence of God's Spirit within the homemaker.* Regardless of neighborhood, busyness, or budget, it's a Spirit-filled homemaker that makes the home a place of peace.

The Bible says it's out of the abundance of the heart that the mouth speaks and produces good things (Luke 6:45), and so orders our homes.

Is there peace in your home? Is there an absence of chaos? Is there order? Is it a place, regardless of how busy, harried, and boisterous, of rest? You know what I'm talking about.

THE INVITATION

Here's what it comes down to: Is the abundance of your heart filled with the Spirit of God? As you pray today, ask yourself, am I ordering my home by some impersonal "Christian checklist" of dos or don'ts, or am I ordering my home out of the abundance of peace that's flowing from my Spirit-filled heart? Is the order coming from my mind or my heart? There's a big difference.

DIVINE REFLECTION AND PRAYER

In the space below, and in your own hand, write out Isaiah 32:18. As you do, reflect upon the invitation, and pray.

Connecting With Your Tribe

YOUR FOURTH MOVE

The focus in the fourth move shifts to people outside of our homes. These are the people we love who don't live with us but are still part of the fabric of our lives. Starting with the people closest to us and moving out from there, our closest friends and extended family are our destination. Sometimes we have friends with whom we have closer relationships than with our blood relatives. This is actually quite common.

Jesus had three disciples who were considered his inner circle. This move invites us to pray for the people in our inner circle. They're in our inner circle usually because they've been there for us. We've trusted them with important decisions. We've been vulnerable and transparent with them in our struggles. Now it's our turn to be there for them.

Extended family are the members of our family with whom we share a blood connection but don't live with us. They're our grandparents, cousins, nieces and nephews, siblings, and others. This includes them and their families. There's much to pray for here. If we can trust God to do it, and expect him to do so, his Spirit will reveal to us exactly how to pray for them. These next six devotions show us how to pray for friends and extended family.

Day 17

BROTHERLY AFFECTION

Love one another with brotherly affection. Outdo one another in showing honor.

ROMANS 12:10 (ESV)

There are all kinds of relationships but only one kind of Christian love.

Relationships vary in degree, but Christian love remains constant throughout the degrees. The love of Christ that is shown in the immediate family of parents and kids is the same love that is shown to extended family and friends. It's also the same love shown to acquaintances, coworkers, neighbors, strangers, and enemies.

What kind of love is this? It's agape love. It's the kind of love that Christ has, and it's the essence of who he is. He's the source. Agape love has little to do with feelings and everything to do with sacrifice and preference. It's a love that sees all people as spiritual kin and demonstrates the honor and respect for them that comes with it.

Christians are the only people who have this kind of love. The world needs it. Every created soul craves it. God, the God of grace, created every person to have an insatiable desire for this kind of love. It's innate. It's undeniable. It's compulsory. We're lost and incomplete without it. The need for it generates the most beautiful, grace-filled, constant, and instinctual search for fulfillment. Many people search their whole lives and never find it.

For some of the people you know, *you're it*. You're the only one in their life who's got it. You're their only hope.

THE INVITATION

Who, in your extended family and friends, is coming to mind right now as you read this? Take note of these precious souls and start pressing in for them. Someone, at some point, did the same thing for you. Today is a great opportunity to "pay it forward."

DIVINE REFLECTION AND PRAYER

In the space below, and in your own hand, write out Romans 12:10. As you do, reflect upon the invitation, and pray.

Day 18

LOVE HAS A FACE

A friend loves at all times, and a brother is born for adversity.
PROVERBS 17:17 (ESV)

Love is actualized in presence. With friends, it's easy to be there when times are good. Everyone loves these times of shared affinities, laughter, memories, great food. . .all that good stuff. Thank God for friends!

Being there in times of need takes friendships to a whole different place. Here's a convenient truth: Adversity is the breeding ground for new life. Faith is born here. Family is born here. Adversity becomes the womb of unbreakable bonds between friends.

The Bible says we're created in God's image. That means we're relational. We need God. We need each other. At no other times is this truer than in times of hardship. Adversity can be our greatest tutor, showing us and helping us reflect God's image. We actually look more like Jesus on the other side of it.

New life is born when we enter the suffering of a friend. Hope materializes. Oxygen flows. Direction comes into view. Love has a face here, it's yours. Love has a name here, it's Jesus.

THE INVITATION

Is it possible that some of your friends and extended family are in the thick of it right now? Today, pray for God's wisdom in knowing how to be there for them and make a fresh commitment to enter in.

DIVINE REFLECTION AND PRAYER

In the space below, and in your own hand, write out Proverbs 17:17. As you do, reflect upon the invitation, and pray.

Day 19

A COOL DRINK

Bear one another's burdens, and so fulfill the law of Christ.
GALATIANS 6:2 (ESV)

The Bible says Jesus came to fulfill the Law of the Old Testament, but he also came to inaugurate a radical new covenant with a new law. Where the Old Testament Law was written in stone, the law of Christ is written on our hearts.

All those Old Testament sacrifices that once involved animals are now living sacrifices, meaning us, our entire body, soul, and spirit.

Most importantly, where the Spirit of God was with man in the Old Testament, the Spirit of God now dwells within man. . .and so completes the law of Christ being written on our hearts. The law of Christ is love.

Bearing one another's burdens, as Christ bore ours, is a great way to be Jesus to others. *Bearing burdens is a sacrificial move.* It means we're giving something up to help.

This kind of sacrifice is found in the giving of time and in the occupation of heart space. It's an incarnational move out of your world and into their world of suffering. The move actualizes a divine solidarity. An intertwining of the hearts communicates that if they're suffering, you're suffering.

THE INVITATION

Who, among those we love, are carrying a burden today? Can you identify one thing you can do to help bear that burden? This might be a phone call or a text of encouragement, a cup of coffee, or a tank of gas for their car. That one thing, no matter how insignificant it might seem to you, will be a cool drink for them. Go do it.

DIVINE REFLECTION AND PRAYER

In the space below, and in your own hand, write out Galatians 6:2. As you do, reflect upon the invitation, and pray.

Day 20

THE LABOR OF NEW LIFE

Two are better than one, because they have a good reward for their toil. For if they fall, one will lift up his fellow. But woe to him who is alone when he falls and has not another to lift him up!
ECCLESIASTES 4:9–10 (ESV)

Here's some good news: All new life comes through labor! Ask any mom. She'll tell you. Threaten to harm her kid, she won't think twice about harming you. Why? She labored hard for that life and no one's going to take it! She values and loves that life so much that she's willing to give up her own life to protect it.

And here's the most powerful part of this truth. Most moms will tell you that giving birth changes them forever. Something in them dies as this new life is brought into theirs. And this dying to self continues as the care for their child never ceases.

Gone forever are the days of living only for herself. Here to stay are the days of providing, protecting, caring, and nurturing for new life. Every day forward is a new sacrifice.

Oftentimes when we're feeling the fatigue of inner labor it means birth of new life is near.

It's true that labor and birthing takes everything we've got and then some. It's a time of grabbing the hand of the one next to us, getting our focal point, and breathing through.

THE INVITATION

Today, as we pray for extended family and friends, is there anyone you know that is laboring right now that could use your hand? Today might be a good day to call them.

DIVINE REFLECTION AND PRAYER

In the space below, and in your own hand, write out Ecclesiastes 4:9–10. As you do, reflect upon the invitation, and pray.

Day 21

DINNER WITH FRIENDS

Do not be deceived: "Bad company ruins good morals."
1 CORINTHIANS 15:33 (ESV)

Let's not be naïve. Let's not be foolish. If we're hanging out with the wrong people, those people have the power to destroy our faith!

When I was a kid people would come over for dinner and my parents would say, "We're having company." I always loved these nights. The grown-ups sat around eating and talking while me and the other kids were playing and having a great time.

For my parents, the meals were relational investments. Underneath the laughter and the chatter, powerful dynamics were at work. Bonds of relationship were being strengthened. Heart strings were intertwining. "We're not alone. We have friends. There is hope." These were the unspoken, life-communicating messages of "having company."

"Having company" with Christians strengthens faith and helps us become better believers. Having wrong company destroys faith and weakens Christian morals.

Here's the principle: Bad people don't destroy faith. *Bad company destroys faith.* Investments into bad relationships work against us. Are we having company with the wrong people?

Jesus ate with sinners, prostitutes, and tax-gatherers, but the company was one-sided. These were not meals of mutual exchange. Jesus wasn't seeking life here; he was giving life. He was giving love. He was in the world, but He was not of the world. You carry the agape love of Christ.

THE INVITATION

Who among your extended family and friends needs an invitation to dinner? Maybe it's time to have company. What night this week or next would be good to have them over?

DIVINE REFLECTION AND PRAYER

In the space below, and in your own hand, write out 1 Corinthians 15:33. As you do, reflect upon the invitation, and pray.

Day 22

THANK GOD FOR GOOD FRIENDS!

Oil and perfume make the heart glad, and the sweetness of a friend comes from his earnest counsel.

PROVERBS 27:9 (ESV)

Only a real friend can give it to us straight. Only real friends can love us enough to speak truth, even when it hurts. They know we might be offended. They know we might be mad. That doesn't stop them. They love us enough to take our ire if that's what's needed for us to walk in truth.

There's no room for formality in these kinds of conversations. There's no observation of social rules like, "You don't knock on someone's door at ten o'clock at night." There's no makeup or hairspray here. Truth needs to be spoken and nothing else matters.

These are the times when a friend loves us enough to drag us into the light. Truth comes like a splash of cold water. Concern shows up to slap us back into reality. This is what love looks like. Thank God for good friends!

And when that divine moment hits where the darkness of our ignorance and stubbornness is pierced by the persistence of their love, the tears of contrition pay homage to this truth. They were right. We were in trouble. We didn't see it. They did. They loved us enough to speak up. We are so blessed. Thank God for good friends!

THE INVITATION

Are you relationally rich? Co-suffering, listening, time, truth, counsel, tears, hugs, slapping, and laughing. . .these are the currencies of good friends. Today, as you pray for them, thank God for how they've been there for you! Ask God to bless them and to help you be an even better friend in return.

DIVINE REFLECTION AND PRAYER

In the space below, and in your own hand, write out Proverbs 27:9. As you do, reflect upon the invitation, and pray.

Worshiping in the Tabernacle

YOUR FIFTH MOVE

The fifth move delivers the believer into the holy sanctuary, the tabernacle. The tabernacle is the gathering place for worship. In the Old Testament the wandering Jews worshiped in a temporary tent structure, until later when the Temple was constructed during the days of King Solomon, and they had a permanent place for worship. In the early days of the church, the believers would often gather in the Temple and in their homes. Corporate worship took place in dedicated spaces.

Why is the fifth move necessary? What is about our church that needs prayer? Isn't everything all holy and happy there? It's not the buildings of our churches that need prayer. It's the pastors and the ministries flowing out of them that need prayer. God is doing something through the worshiping local pastor. God is doing something through the worshiping local church. Up-reach to God gives birth to outreach to the community. The battle is intense, and the resistance is fierce.

The local pastor needs prayer. Pastors often hear people ask them to pray for them but rarely are they asked how they can be prayed for. Here's the truth about the struggles facing the common local pastor: most live in pressure cookers that induce continuous levels of exhaustion and stress; most live "on call" twenty-four hours a day, seven days per week; most live with conflict within their churches; and most live with a constant feeling of being overwhelmed.

Pastors are not perfect. They're regular people who God called into ministry. Usually this is not a compliment because God only chooses the broken ones he knows will rely upon him. Most are imperfect, battle-scarred, and contend with low self-worthiness on a regular basis. As one with several years of experience, I can testify that pastors are a work in progress. They're always in a state of transition and their calling places large targets on their backs.

Pastors are not the only people to consider in the local church. The ministries that flow out of the church, and the people leading them, need prayer. As much as the devil targets the pastors, the in-reach and out-reach ministries of the local church are also regularly targeted. The devil will do anything to thwart the effectiveness of these services. They need prayer. The vision and mission of the church in one hand with the Bible in the other equips the believer to join the Spirit in praying for them.

If there were one component of the local church that provides the greatest risk to its effectiveness in the worship of God and the outreach to the community, it's the members. Jesus spent most of his ministry with the poor, blind, lame, and crippled. These were the rejected cast-aways of society who not only needed the love and hope of Jesus Christ. They were starved for it. When they got it, they left everything to follow after him. This dynamic hasn't changed. The church is full of them, me included. Many of the church's conflicts flow out of the fumbles of less-than-perfect moments of such precious souls.

The only hope to overcome these dynamics is the mutual grace being exchanged through relationships centered on Christ. "Koinonia" is the Greek word for this kind of fellowship between believers. Jesus is at the center. Relationships flow through him where agape love covers a multitude of sins. The fifth move invites you to pray for your pastor, the ministries of your church, and the fellowship of believers in your church. These next six devotions will show you how to pray for them.

Day 23

ACTIVE WORSHIP

For where two or three gather in my name, there am I with them.
MATTHEW 18:20 (NIV)

The Greek word for "gather" describes a coming together with the intent of worship. It's a powerful guarantee that when the body of Christ comes together to worship Jesus, he promises to be there.

Do you believe this promise? Two questions need answers. One, what does it mean to worship? And, what does it mean that Jesus is there?

Worship is more than song. Worship is also the proclamation of the Gospel. When I'm preaching, I'm worshiping. So is the congregation when they're participating.

The Spirit is at work. The word of Truth, alive and active, is cutting, piercing, judging hearts, convicting, and imparting life. I don't know about anybody else, but I feel it when I've been cut. I feel it when I'm being convicted. I feel it when God's righteousness has been divinely injected into my spirit! I respond when stuff like this happens. Sometimes I cry. Sometimes I beat my chest. Sometimes I shout.

This is active worship. This is actively participating in the sermon. This is what Jesus meant when he said, "I am with them." He is here. His Spirit is moving. His bride is responding. Our response, our participation, is our testimony. God is real. I am being healed. I am being delivered. I am being transformed. I am a new creation.

THE INVITATION

What are the areas your church needs prayer today? Pray for your pastor and leaders. Pray for your members. Pray for those yet to come. Pray that you will be a worshiper that participates in the proclamation of God's word!

DIVINE REFLECTION AND PRAYER

In the space below, and in your own hand, write out Matthew 18:20. As you do, reflect upon the invitation, and pray.

Day 24

A GOOD STIR

And let us consider how to stir up one another to love and good works, not neglecting to meet together, as is the habit of some, but encouraging one another, and all the more as you see the Day drawing.

HEBREWS 10:24–25 (ESV)

How many times do we find ourselves stirring up the wrong stuff. . .the wrong social media post, the wrong comment to someone we love, the wrong reaction, or how about this one, the wrong thoughts toward someone? This kind of stirring comes way too easy for human nature.

The biblical word for "stir" here means to agitate, provoke, incite, or "jab" someone so they must respond. How about this twist, what if someone jabbed us to do good, to use our spiritual gifts and fruit? How much of our fruit has fallen to the ground only to rot away? How many times has our gift gone unused?

Or, what would it look like if we were the one doing the provoking? *This is good stirring.* This is the kind of stirring we can do all day long. Finally, a legitimate reason to nag the people we love!

Stirring is supposed to be a normal activity in a community of faith, in the context of worship. Spiritual gifts and fruit are for believers; to be shared with each other, to help us become better, stronger believers. Stirring one another to use them makes the church stronger.

Let's not be chintzy with our fruit and gifts! That stuff is not for us. It's for them. It's for others. They need it. It's God's design for us to share.

THE INVITATION

What are your spiritual gifts? Today, as you pray for our church community, ask God to help you be a better fruit and gift sharer. Go to church. Share the love. Nag a friend.

DIVINE REFLECTION AND PRAYER

In the space below, and in your own hand, write out Hebrews 10:24–25. As you do, reflect upon the invitation, and pray.

Day 25

ONE BREAD, ONE BODY

Because there is one bread, we who are many are one body, for we all partake of the one bread.
1 CORINTHIANS 10:17 (ESV)

Communion was a full meal in the earliest centuries of the church. But it wasn't just for eating. When it came time to share the event, the believers would shift into a deeper state of worship, a particularly sacred, contemplative, and participative space.

The early believers believed the presence of Christ was there and that the meal had become a sacrament. The bread was his body. The wine, his blood.

Yes, his sacrifice was remembered. Yes, thanksgiving was poured out. But the partaking was not just recollection and exaltation; it was a mutual sharing in what had been accomplished on the cross.

His death is mine. I am not who I used to be. His resurrection is mine. I am a new creation. I am with him. He is in me. We are one. Divine "re-membering" was taking place.

His death is ours. We are not who we used to be. His resurrection is ours. We are a new creation. We are in him. He is in us. We are one.

THE INVITATION

Are you all in with your church? Are you part of the one? You know your pastor's there for you, right? You know you are loved, right? What about the others? Do they know you're there for them? Do they know you love them?

Today's a good day to pray for oneness, unity, and strength. Let's do this.

DIVINE REFLECTION AND PRAYER

In the space below, and in your own hand, write out I Corinthians 10:17. As you do, reflect upon the invitation, and pray.

Day 26

LOVE AT RISK

Therefore, confess your sins to one another and pray for one another, that you may be healed. The prayer of a righteous person has great power as it is working.

JAMES 5:16 (ESV)

Confessing sins to another person is tough! If I'm already struggling with the shame fallout of sin, why would I want to share that with others?

"So, let me get this straight, Jesus: I committed a sin; I feel the weight of shame, and at the very moment that I want to go hide in a hole, you're telling me I need to go show this stuff to someone and have them pray for me? Is this correct?"

"Yes."

"Isn't this a little sadistic?"

"Not if you want to be healed. I know you're hurting. I was there. I saw it. I know you're wanting to avoid me and others. I know what you're covered in. I know you're longing for darkness. But this is the way out. I'm the only one who can fix this. I'm the only one who can forgive you and cleanse you and bring healing to the sickness that's causing you to sin."

"But if I confess this to someone, won't they think I'm a horrible person? And, what if they turn on me and use the information against me?"

"They might. Love is a risk. Trust me, I know about this risk. And, no. They won't think bad of you. Not in a million years. You're helping them. There's a blessing I give with this kind of trust. I'm there when this is happening. I'm moving. Change is taking place. For both of you."

"So, you're telling me my brokenness and my vulnerability helps *them* with their faith?"

"Exactly. How could it not? I'm there. You're there. They're praying. Great things happen when people pray."

THE INVITATION

Who do you trust for this kind of prayer and vulnerability? Today, thank God for the good souls you can trust and be vulnerable with for prayer.

DIVINE REFLECTION AND PRAYER

In the space below, and in your own hand, write out James 5:16. As you do, reflect upon the invitation, and pray.

Day 27

OH, HOW HE LOVES US!

I was glad when they said to me, "Let us go to the house of the Lord!"

PSALM 122:1 (ESV)

David really loved God. He not only belonged to God; he was smitten by him. His heart lit up at the thought of worship. His emotions swelled with gladness.

What was his secret? Where did he get this kind of love and why did he love going to church so much?

Here's a principle: the key for a love of going to church is not knowing how much we love God; *it's knowing how much God loves us.*

Do you believe God loves you? Has this truth become a permanent fixture in the deepest part of your heart?

This is the biggest truth that happens in a person's life. It's the difference between knowing *about* God's love and *experiencing* God's love. It's the truth that happens only in the context of worship.

So here's the irony to David's secret: David knew how much God loved him because of how much he worshiped God.

Here's the beauty of this divine irony: It takes only the slightest spark to get this love cycle started. Those who left everything to follow Jesus were the ones in the crowds. *They showed up.* They were there. It's the only way they could have experienced the truth of God's love for them.

THE INVITATION

Are you all in with your church? We will never love God like David if we're not all in. It's time to get back to church!

DIVINE REFLECTION AND PRAYER

In the space below, and in your own hand, write out Psalm 122:1. As you do, reflect upon the invitation, and pray.

Day 28

THE LIVING BODY

Now you are the body of Christ and individually members of it.
1 CORINTHIANS 12:27 (ESV)

Christ was a real historical person who lived and died and rose again. Though the world cannot see the historical Jesus anymore, it can see his church. That's us!

If anyone has met any of my kids, they've met me. When they talk with them, they see them and hear them with all their personalities and interests, and all that good stuff, but they also see me. (Of course all the good stuff in my kids comes from their mother!).

Let me ask you this, when people talk with you, are they seeing Christ in you?

To the unbeliever, Christ is seen as the living presentation of the gospel message. "I was dead but now I am alive." "I was blind but now I see." "I used to be lost without hope but now I am found and I have purpose."

The Christian is a walking billboard of the hope found in Jesus Christ.

To the believer, Christ is seen in the spiritual gifts and fruit. The Spirit builds and equips the church with these things. Each person is an individual part of the body of Christ and necessary for its health and function.

THE INVITATION

Are you doing your part in the body of Christ? Or have you become lame? In other words, have you become a withered hand or a withered foot? Today, let's pray that each person in the church is a strong and healthy member, including you. The church needs you.

DIVINE REFLECTION AND PRAYER

In the space below, and in your own hand, write out 1 Corinthians 12:27. As you do, reflect upon the invitation, and pray.

Showing Love in the Marketplace

YOUR SIXTH MOVE

The focal point of this move is community. The marketplace consists of all the people, places, and organizations we're involved with outside of the home and church. This includes our job, social circles, classmates, stores and restaurants we visit with regularity.

Most of us have a rhythm to our life that brings us into contact with the same people and places on a regular basis. We drive the same routes, stopping at the same places for gasoline, convenience stores, grocery stores, and restaurants. Faces become familiar. The same people working the same shifts. Sometimes we arrive at a first-name basis with these precious people. As Jesus left heaven to enter our world, so the believer makes the same incarnational prayer move into the lives of our marketplace people.

Coworker relationships are unique. We usually know a great deal of information about our boss and coworkers. The same goes with our classmates at school. Micro-comments appear in little conversations that flash insights into what's really happening in their lives. Sometimes these are cries for help. Sometimes they are invitations for the relationship to go deeper.

I became friends with several people at a dog park I used to visit several times per week. I was there on the same days and times along with the other people doing the same thing. Many of them visited my church. A few of them I'm still friends with several years later even though I no longer go to the dog park. I've learned how my prayers for them changed our relationships.

The Bible says Jesus died for the sins of the whole world. God wants all people to come to repentance. The Spirit is at work drawing all people to Christ. Most believers have people who went before them, praying them into the Kingdom. Some of these could have been people who knew them from the marketplace. Where might the Spirit be moving in our marketplaces? This sixth move, spread out over the next six devotions, directs our prayers to the needs of the people in our marketplace.

Day 29

WRECKING BALL LOVE

And he said to him, "You shall love the Lord your God with all your heart and with all your soul and with all your mind. This is the great and first commandment. And a second is like it: You shall love your neighbor as yourself. On these two commandments depend all the Law and the Prophets."

MATTHEW 22:37–40 (ESV)

Love God. Love others. This is it. This sums up the entire Bible. Two phrases. The whole thing, cover to cover, neatly packaged.

The Greek word for "love" in these verses is "agape." Agape love is the kind of love that we cannot manufacture on our own. It's not found anywhere on earth. It's otherworldly, transcendent, indescribable. It's divine. It's not a commodity.

Agape love has very little to do with us, our feelings, and our emotions, and everything to do with the sacrifice and service to others. It means our best shot, our best attempt, our only hope at loving God and others, is doomed without it.

God is such a genius! *His greatest commands cannot be fulfilled without him!* Jesus loves us with this kind of love. He fills us with it. And the "it," by the way, is him. Jesus doesn't have agape love. He is agape love.

The love we need to love God and others is the very presence of Jesus in us.

THE INVITATION

What does love for others look like when it's agape love? How can we love our community this week? If you want to be a better lover of others, you need to be better loved. *This is on you.* This is your move. He's already made his. Loving others begins by being loved first by Christ. Press in. Get wrecked. And become a wrecking ball.

DIVINE REFLECTION AND PRAYER

In the space below, and in your own hand, write out Matthew 22:37–40. As you do, reflect upon the invitation, and pray.

Day 30

A PRAYER FOR OUR NEIGHBORHOOD

But seek the welfare of the city where I have sent you into exile, and pray to the LORD on its behalf, for in its welfare you will find your welfare.

JEREMIAH 29:7 (ESV)

Jeremiah was God's prophet during the time of Babylonian captivity. And even though Israel was in trouble, God never abandoned his relationship with them. He kept speaking to them.

One of his messages was for the Israelites to seek the welfare for the city in which they would live during the exile. God was saying, "Your survival depends on them. Your welfare depends on their welfare."

The Israelites' success during the exile was dependent not on them praying for themselves, but for how they were praying for others.

If Jeremiah showed up in our churches today he would have the same message for us. He would tell us to pray for our community. The prayer is not for us to grow; it's for them to grow. It's not for us to be blessed; it's for them to be blessed.

More pointedly, he would say, "Go be Jesus to your community. Pray for them. Be there for them. Help them. You're the keepers of the blessing. Go love them. Go share it. Frequent their businesses. Support their schools. This is the stuff God blesses."

THE INVITATION

Who are the people you normally interact with in the marketplace? What are some specific ways you can pray for them today?

DIVINE REFLECTION AND PRAYER

In the space below, and in your own hand, write out Jeremiah 29:7. As you do, reflect upon the invitation, and pray.

Day 31

MAKING THE CUT

O Lord, who shall sojourn in your tent? Who shall dwell on your holy hill? He who walks blamelessly and does what is right and speaks truth in his heart; who does not slander with his tongue and does no evil to his neighbor, nor takes up a reproach against his friend;

PSALM 15:1–3 (ESV)

A question of belonging. A question of abiding. Who are the ones that will dine with the Lord? Who are the ones who will sleep in God's tent?

David knew the answer. *They would be the ones who share God's heart to the greatest degree.* They would be the ones who know the way of Christ and who walk it well. They are the ones whose words and actions are right. They are honest in their thoughts. They don't say bad things about their neighbors or devise evil plans against them.

Sharing God's heart. Loving others.

Here's a truth: we can never go wrong by sharing the love of Jesus to our neighbors and friends! We may stumble in our delivery. We may slip up and look a little silly sometimes. We may have offered something that wasn't needed. None of this stuff matters.

What matters is that the love of Jesus reached out and touched someone.

THE INVITATION

Do you believe this? The love of God never returns void. That's the truth. Let's change someone's world today with the love of Christ!

DIVINE REFLECTION AND PRAYER

In the space below, and in your own hand, write out Psalm 15:1–3. As you do, reflect upon the invitation, and pray.

Day 32

THREE POWERFUL WORDS

There is only one lawgiver and judge, he who is able to save and to destroy. But who are you to judge your neighbor?
JAMES 4:12 (ESV)

Judgment is reserved for the one who has all the facts. This is not us, by the way. Only God has all the facts. We rarely have all the facts. And yet, we judge! How many times have we settled in on a judgment about one of our neighbors only to discover our facts were wrong? I think this happens way more than we think.

Cleaning up these messes requires two messages: One, "I'm sorry" and, two, 'will you forgive me?' The first is an admission of guilt; the second is a request for reconciliation.

The best way to avoid judging others is to first ask, is this really any of my business? Many of our sinful lapses into judging others can be avoided by honestly answering this question. Secondly, if it is a matter that requires our involvement, one small phrase, of three powerful words, can quickly diffuse animosity, "Help me understand."

One clear and incontrovertible fact rises to the top when dealing with conflicts with others: We don't have all the facts. Let's let every action be safeguarded by a commitment that we will not take action until we are certain we have enough information. And when we think we're ready to move, let's pray and follow the guidelines set forth in Matthew 18.

THE INVITATION

Is there someone you need to ask, "Help me understand?" Instead of judging them; help them. Be Jesus to them. How can you pray for them today?

DIVINE REFLECTION AND PRAYER

In the space below, and in your own hand, write out James 4:12. As you do, reflect upon the invitation, and pray.

Day 33

BEING WITNESSES

But you will receive power when the Holy Spirit comes upon you. And you will be my witnesses, telling people about me everywhere—in Jerusalem, throughout Judea, in Samaria, and to the ends of the earth."
ACTS 1:8 (NLT)

From Pastor Stacy Valenzuela.
As neighbors we have a unique opportunity and even privilege to have a voice in the lives of people who live life in the same places we do.

In a way, we live in a cul-de-sac rich with opportunity. We have amazing and hardworking single parents, people with discouraging health issues, widows, Christians and non-Christians. These beautiful people are our people. Some of us are in each other's business, some of us chat only when we happen to pull into our driveways at the same time, and some of us only see each other when we have a holiday block party. But guess what, we are neighbors and there is a God-given love that our family has for the others and I believe that they have for us. When tragedy strikes, we love hard.

When there is good news, we celebrate with each other. For such a time as this, we are called to be neighbors to these people.

God sees inside their walls just as He sees inside ours. He knows every fight that has been fought, every tear that has been cried, and every heart that has sought help inside those walls. But we don't know all those things. We don't need to know all those things. All we need to know is that God called us to be neighbors to these people. He called us to love these people—even the ones that don't seem to want our love. He has called us His witnesses and said that we start here.

We get to love one another by being neighborly. We can bring meals, sit for a cup of coffee, leave notes, etc. We can build relationships with those who live right beside us. At some point, love for these people overwhelms us and we can't help but "tell people about [Him] everywhere." We see God's hand in choosing us for our neighborhood. We mustn't delay in being the literal neighbor that God intended us to be.

THE INVITATION

Which one of your neighbors needs some loving today? Bring flowers (doesn't have to be fancy—you could pick one from your yard—or even your neighbor's yard. Just joking. Don't do that.), say hello and walk over instead of hurrying inside, leave a note complimenting a neighbor on something you like about their home.

DIVINE REFLECTION AND PRAYER

In the space below, and in your own hand, write out Acts 1:8. As you do, reflect upon the invitation, and pray.

Day 34

THE OUCH OF FORGIVENESS

Do not seek revenge or bear a grudge against anyone among your people, but love your neighbor as yourself. I am the LORD.
LEVITICUS 19:18 (NIV)

The Bible tells us a few things about grudges. First, as Christians, we're going to experience wrongs being done to us. This comes with the territory. I think we need to wrap our minds around this once and for all and get it settled. *If you belong to Jesus, the devil's going to try and take you out.*

Second, the Bible tells us when these things happen, we're not allowed to stew about them and hold ill feelings toward the person who did us harm.

There's a couple of reasons why the Lord requires this extra mile from us. It's a matter of the heart. Willful harboring of grudges in our hearts is the antithesis of what it means to be a Christian. Doing so not only forces a stop between us and the person but it also remains lodged in our hearts affecting literally everything else we think, say, or do.

A grudge says, "I refuse to forgive this person." But, Jesus said we're not allowed to walk in his forgiveness and refuse to forgive others. He made that very clear.

Holding a grudge prevents us from turning that person over to God because we're still holding on. Trusting God with our hurt and the person who hurt us sets us free. Forgiveness is surrendering them to the only Judge who is truly just. God doesn't wink at sin, it's not fair to the victims. Those who stand before the Lord will get what they deserve.

THE INVITATION

Who's coming to your mind right now? I have a few. Do the right thing today and start asking God to help you forgive them. Get the poison out of your heart. Ask God to help you start loving them like you love yourself.

DIVINE REFLECTION AND PRAYER

In the space below, and in your own hand, write out Leviticus 19:18. As you do, reflect upon the invitation, and pray.

Going to the Highways and Byways

YOUR SEVENTH MOVE

The seventh move to simplify prayer transports us beyond our marketplaces to the highways and byways of the world around us. Here the zones of the unfamiliar people and places come into view. These are the desolate places of the castaways, forgotten, and ghosted...those we have a hard time loving or liking. This also includes our civic leaders, political issues, the need for prayer from natural disasters, and the victims of evil around the world. All who, if not for the incarnational love of Christ pulsating in the hearts of praying believers, may never have anyone praying for them.

Interceding for people with whom we've never met can be challenging. How do we pray passionately for people we don't know? Jesus said, "With man this is impossible, but with God, all things are possible" (Matthew 19:26). One of the things I've come to understand about prayer is how fluent prayer becomes when we quit trying to pray out of knowledge and instead join in the prayers already taking place in the heavens. Like singing along with the chorus of a favorite song, Spirit-led prayer allows the believer to pray with familiarity in the places of unfamiliarity.

God has a heart for the people no one cares about. In the Old Testament, God made laws that guaranteed that widows, orphans, and immigrants would be taken care of. Jesus spent nearly all his ministering with this same group of people. In the New Testament, they are referred to as the poor, the blind, the lame, and the crippled. Same people. What do they all have in common? If no one helps them, they will not survive. The gospel of Luke tells us this is the mission of the Holy Spirit (4:18).

This last move, and our final six devotions, escorts us into the dire circumstances of the places of broken people where the Spirit of God is needed to bring about healing and deliverance. Let's join in the mission of the Spirit by praying for the lost to be found and for the name of Jesus to be exalted.

Day 35

THE RIPE HARVEST

Then he said to his disciples, "The harvest is plentiful, but the laborers are few; therefore pray earnestly to the Lord of the harvest to send out laborers into his harvest."

MATTHEW 9:37–38 (ESV)

By the time Jesus made this comment, he had just come off spending a great amount of time ministering in the villages. The people were in bad shape. They were lost and beat up. He said they were like sheep without a shepherd.

What would a sheep look like without a shepherd? It wouldn't last long, that's for sure! Having no shepherd would mean having no food, no water, no protection against predators, no comforting voice of authority, no balm for their injuries, and no rest for their weariness.

The Bible says Jesus was filled with compassion for them. He sat with them and talked with them. His words were living bread and water for their famished and parched spirits. His words were a barrier of truth. They were protected. On the inside, the people were safe with the Shepherd. On the outside were the frustrated predators, stymied dejectedly by the Shepherd's care. His words were comforting. They were not alone. They belonged. His hands brought healing balm from their sicknesses and diseases. They were whole. They were healed.

It must have been exhausting for Jesus; not the work but the volume of work. His command to his disciples? Pray for more laborers. There was too much harvest and not enough harvesters!

Do we think it's any different today? Not a chance. The harvest is even greater! As Christians, we are called to pray for laborers and we are called to be laborers. The work is easy. How hard is it to pick fruit ripe for the harvest?

THE INVITATION

How do we do that? We do what Jesus did. We open our eyes to the lost and the beat-up condition of the poor souls around us. We get wrecked by it. Then, instinctually, compulsively, we go. We talk. We touch.

DIVINE REFLECTION AND PRAYER

In the space below, and in your own hand, write out Matthew 9:37–38. As you do, reflect upon the invitation, and pray.

Day 36

RIGHT PLACE. RIGHT TIME.

But he went out and began to talk freely about it, and to spread the news, so that Jesus could no longer openly enter a town, but was out in desolate places, and people were coming to him from every quarter.

MARK 1:45 (ESV)

It only took short time for Jesus' ministry to become so popular that he was forced to minister only in the outskirts of the towns. The crowds were too large. The mayhem was too disruptive. This worked out perfectly for Jesus. All the people who needed Jesus were there. The outskirts of town is where all the lepers, the unclean, the homeless, and the castaways lived.

In the Gospels, these people were called the poor, the blind, the lame, and the crippled. In the Old Testament, they were called the widows, the orphans, and the immigrants. It was the same group of people. They all had one thing in common: If not for the charity of others, they would die.

God had a special place in his heart for them. In the Old Testament God commanded Moses to create special laws for the Israelites to take care of them. In the New Testament, Jesus, empowered by the Holy Spirit, focused most of his attention on them.

God's heart has not changed for these precious souls. Those who need Jesus the most are those who are on the outside, hurting, embarrassed, and disconnected. These are the ones who've pulled away. They've self-banished themselves to the disparity of the fringes. Sometimes they front bravado to hide their brokenness. Other times they're so downtrodden that they've lost all hope.

What's the good news in all of this? These precious souls are so easy to love. So easy. Just a few moments of being Jesus to them can literally change them forever.

THE INVITATION

Who are the poor, the blind, the lame, the crippled, and, the widow, the orphans, and the immigrants in your life? Today, say a prayer for them. Maybe you can help. Maybe you can be Jesus to them.

DIVINE REFLECTION AND PRAYER

In the space below, and in your own hand, write out Mark 1:4–5. As you do, reflect upon the invitation, and pray.

Day 37

THE SEEDBED OF OPPORTUNITY

For I am not ashamed of the gospel, for it is the power of God for salvation to everyone who believes, to the Jew first and also to the Greek.

ROMANS 1:16 (ESV)

This was a big statement for the Apostle Paul. He was once the guy who persecuted the church and who was putting the gospel to shame. Now he was the guy who was proud of the gospel. What happened?

He met Jesus, that's what happened! That's all it takes. One genuine encounter with Jesus. It's hard to imagine a person who was more against the Christian faith than Paul. And, yet he was converted and completely transformed. Here's a comforting truth: *The hardest of hearts, with even the greatest of offense toward the gospel, are never out of reach of the touch of Jesus Christ.*

Do we have a Paul somewhere in our lives? Do we have someone who is actively rejecting the gospel? Never give up hope. Never quit praying. Never quit being Jesus to them. They're never out of reach.

What can we do? Our part in their life is twofold: One, never be ashamed of them, and, two, never be ashamed of the gospel. That is, never be ashamed of our testimony of how God saved us. This is the best version of the gospel you will ever share!

How do we do this with the Pauls in our lives? This is surprisingly and remarkably easy. *Timing is everything.* Brokenness is the perfect seedbed for sowing seeds. This is what we look for. We become evangelistically opportunistic! We pray for them, love them, and keep reaching out to them. Then, when brokenness strikes, we move in with the seeds of hope. They're ready. There's no guarantee that the perfect timing will always deliver immediate results, but that doesn't stop us. Seeds have been planted.

THE INVITATION

Who are the broken people in your life that need your connection? Today, pray for God to stir within you a plan to help them.

DIVINE REFLECTION AND PRAYER

In the space below, and in your own hand, write out Romans 1:16. As you do, reflect upon the invitation, and pray.

Day 38

THIS LITTLE LIGHT OF MINE

In the same way, let your light shine before others, so that they may see your good works and give glory to your Father who is in heaven.

MATTHEW 5:16 (ESV)

I have a light fixture outside my garage that has a short. It works, but the bulb barely puts out any light. If Charlie Brown had a light outside his garage, it would definitely look like mine. Are we like a light fixture with a short? Are we shining in all our capacity?

Before we answer, let's be reminded that *kingdom shining looks nothing like worldly shining*. A couple of things worth noting about kingdom light. One, it's not ours. It has nothing to do with our ability, our personality, our charisma, our charm, good looks, success, our trophies, or our incredible intellect.

If there's any part of us that looks good in the eyes of the world, it's because we've manufactured it ourselves. Talk about a lot of work! How exhausting. And yes, there is a payoff for this kind of worldly light, but its wages are certainly not eternal life.

Second, the light of which Jesus spoke is a light of other-worldly brilliance. It's eternal. It's internal. And it's enviable. Worldly light flows out of body and soul, but kingdom light flows out of spirit. It's a radiance that pulsates from God's abundant riches; an ironic and iconic peace that transcends comprehension.

Third, kingdom light is tapped into the most surprising of power sources. The plug? The excruciating loss of being seen as a big zero in the eyes of the world! A big nothingburger.

THE INVITATION

Do you want to shine brighter? Is it worth it to you? Today, as you pray, ask God to make you invisible in the eyes of the world.

DIVINE REFLECTION AND PRAYER

In the space below, and in your own hand, write out Matthew 5:16. As you do, reflect upon the invitation, and pray.

Day 39

IDENTIFY FIDELITY

For Christ did not send me to baptize but to preach the gospel, and not with words of eloquent wisdom, lest the cross of Christ be emptied of its power.

1 CORINTHIANS 1:17 (ESV)

Paul knew what he was about. He was not a pastor. He was not a prophet. He was not a baptizer. He was an evangelist, teacher, and apostle. He was never in doubt. Never in deception. He could not be tempted to try and be someone he wasn't.

His preaching had no pretense. There was no one to impress. There was no group from which to garner respect. No need for high and lofty words. He ministered truth, in truth.

Are you trying to be someone you're not? When all the layers of self are peeled away, and what's left is the purest essence of our truest God-given identity, who do we see there?

Is this the reality of our self-image?

This is a pretty big deal. Identity fidelity is the packaging of ministry competency. And don't try and tell me you don't have a ministry! Every believer has one! We're here for a reason.

Paul knew all this. He didn't mess around.

THE INVITATION

What about you? Do you know this? Or are you just messing around? Trying to minister through a cloak of self-deception disempowers the presentation of the gospel. The world needs to see the gospel in power. That's you. That's me. But there's no power where there's no truth.

DIVINE REFLECTION AND PRAYER

In the space below, and in your own hand, write out 1 Corinthians 1:17. As you do, reflect upon the invitation, and pray.

Day 40

THE RIGHT MOVE

To the weak I became weak, that I might win against the weak. I have become all things to all people, that by all means I might save some.

1 CORINTHIANS 9:22 (ESV)

Do you see the move Paul was making here? This is the move of incarnational love. There's a divine shift that takes place from the lover to the beloved here. Jesus made this same move when the Word became flesh. He also made it when he washed his disciples' feet. The Bible says he willingly laid down his own clothes to take up the towel of servanthood.

If we want to see someone light up right in front of our eyes, we need to make this move. *We need to move into their space!* This is the gait of agape love. It moves. It shifts. It goes after. It puts on. It goes in.

The payoff of the move is enormous. There's an old maxim that says people don't care how much you know until they know how much you care. This is caring in action. It's a move that delivers agape love like nothing else.

What are some of your favorite memories growing up? I'll bet many of them hinge on times just like this. Someone came into your world. Someone saw you. They saw what you loved. They left their world and came into yours. It was so meaningful that it's still a memory for you today.

THE INVITATION

What was it like when Jesus came into your world? How can you be Jesus to your world today? As we pray for the world around us today, let's be Jesus to them, and make this move.

DIVINE REFLECTION AND PRAYER

In the space below, and in your own hand, write out 1 Corinthians 9:22. As you do, reflect upon the invitation, and pray.

CONCLUSION

My prayer for you during these forty days was that your prayer life would be successfully simplified.

God loves all people. God loves you. His plans for you are to make you prosper. Sometimes God's plans involve some faith storms that help our faith grow. Sometimes God's plans involve seasons of great success. It's all good because it all comes from God.

The moves we encountered in this devotional incarnationally escorted us into the sacred realm of God's plans for ourselves, our families, our friends, our churches, our communities, and our world. The moves helped develop within us a layer of spirit sensitivity to God's plans. These are the best kind of prayers.

The moves begin with worshiping God in the throne room. Next, we lay ourselves on the altar as we pray for ourselves. The next move brings us into our homes where we pray for our immediate family and our closest of relationships.

From here we move out to the people in our tribe. These are those with whom we share life at work, friends and acquaintances, neighbors, etc. The next move brings our focus on to our church. Here our pastors and fellow brothers and sisters in Christ come into view.

After this, the final two moves bring us into the marketplace. These are the precious souls that we're always bumping in to as we shop, frequent restaurants, hit the convenience stores, and all the other places we visit in the rhythm of our lives. The last move brings into focus all the ways we're praying for our surroundings, like our cities and towns, states, country. And the world.

Conclusion

The moves follow a simple trajectory that begins with worship and ends in outreach, the heart of what it means to be a Christian. My prayer is that these moves have helped establish a simple, flowing structure to your prayer life that has made prayer easy.

ABOUT THE AUTHOR

Dr. Jeff McAffee is a full-time pastor. He has degrees in theology and homiletics. He preaches and teaches. He trains ministers. He writes. He teaches college classes. His parishioners call him Pastor. His college students call him Doctor. His friends call him bro, brother, or dude.

Pastor Jeff knows what it's like to struggle in the arena of prayer. . .of wanting to be better but not knowing how to get there. He's learned the value of looking at prayer through seven moves that have radically changed everything.

His wife, Kendra, still loves him after twenty-seven years of marriage. His three kids Ethan, Anna, and Ella are smart, beautiful, love God and others, and have great plans for their futures.

CPSIA information can be obtained
at www.ICGtesting.com
Printed in the USA
JSHW071143050223
37139JS00003B/15